# big bella's dirty cafe

paul summers

dogeater
books that bite

First Published in the UK in 2006 by dogeater
PO Box 990 Newcastle upon Tyne NE99 2US
www.dogeater.co.uk

dogeater is a member of
Independent Northern Publishers
www.northernpublishers.co.uk

Typeset in Garamond

Cover design and typesetting by dogeater

Cover photograph by David Gray
from the artist book *Cunawabi*
courtesy of David Gray
www.cunawabi.com

ISBN 0 9546515 3 7

for Ash

# contents

# fossil
(an egocentric ponders coastal erosion)

a million years down the track,
a portion at least of my petrified
corpse will appear in a cliff face
on the north east coast.

some cute kid, freshly lifted from his dad's
aching shoulders will make the find;
wet his knickers in fright, need months
of counselling just to speak.

i'll be strewn between sticky clay & igneous rock,
my gob open as usual, a little more tanned looking:
preserved, the scientists will later impart,
by high levels of tobacco tar & blended scotch whisky.

my eyes will have dissolved, my lips shrunk to nothing
& my hair will need some serious attention.
but i'm smiling, i'm definitely smiling.
it's unshiftable, like a handsome tomcat's
musky legacy.

# fishing at blyth harbour with jimmy's ghost

paralysed snow slaps
the cold glass of your specs.
the skeletons of tiny fish,
of ant eaten leaves,
the feathers of extinct birds

& you, smiling like harry lime
in the staithes' wet shadows,
our laughter exhaled in whale plumes
fighting the elements to roll a tab
& ten miles out

the grey tumour, sky
slowly growing, puffing out its chest.
the tsunami's nascent trough
snaring frail light
in concave reflections of heaven.

## bird

lunch-time mourners gather,
congealing like storm-cloud
on the wet pavement.
a pigeon, beak bleeding

& broken-winged,
circles like a toreador
in the city's muck.
the man with white hair

steps out from the crowd
& checking around him
for children's eyes,
gently snaps its neck.

## chance encounter

the sun had opened doors,
perched folk reluctantly on steps;
the sales of ice-lollies rocketed.
alice looked tired, greg like a junkie,
cradling a ten-pack of warm dutch dumpies
like the baby they'd talked about
but never gotten round to.

## october song

a full grey mile beneath
the antics of a show-off gull
wet slate slumps in whale-backs
exhausted by the weight of sky
the colour of my mother's eyes

the rumbling belly of a land-bound storm
an echo in a canopy of emptying trees
of childish numbers counted in between
old archie wets a conker with his spit
& polishes it to a racehorse sheen

## school photo

we were deranged looking,
ragged kids in badly fitting blazers,
all skinhead & broken nose,
segged brogues & *Jam* badges.
ours will be different:
not one of them called after a saint -
they will dip their rhubarb into brown sugar.

## team-talk

knees blooded & black with clarts, moist
troops in the reek of liniment & smoke.

the gaffa is steaming, hoofing the kit-bag,
eyes shooting daggers at les, the keeper.

four whole minutes of dry-mouth silence,
then tommy explodes: *absolute shite!*

*every last one of you is playing like a turd!*
*& you les! you're playing worse than shite!*

& us, just slouched, like thirsty leaves,
like heavy corn glimpsing the scythe.

## sniffa's off the glue

he's gone all metaphysical,
wants to be a beachcomber
on some lonely coast, has
taken to collecting discarded
feathers, bits of wood.

debs saw him in the library -
the library! searching for tahiti
in an ancient atlas. sniffa just
winked, ripped out a page &
stuffed it in his carrier, smiling.

dan saw him yesterday, crouched
on the pier, staring hard at the long
horizon, hunting the curve, knowing
that somewhere in the sea's grey haze
the lost arc is cradled by blue.

# driftwood

he is skimming pebbles through rip-tides:
each cold, flat stone, skipping
the sea's relentless beat

on the grey beach at easter,
the young lovers kiss;
their first in daylight,
sober, after nervous breakfasts.

above them, the clouds fidget.

## november song

a red faced woman the shape of an egg
struggles against leans like a ski-jumper
into a gust cold enough to turn this bullet
rain to bitter-tasting snow that so quickly
disappears to swell the spring-tide spittle

pool collected in the hollow of my tongue
the spying mink have powdered their wigs
their manic dances slowed to funeral waltz
an old dog shivers wishes for a pair of shoes
well-made & stitched so tight to keep out

every drop & draught that forces itself on him
& in the mud of most-walked routes a dozen
leaves have formed themselves in celtic knots
a parasite disease illuminates with domino spots
two centuries ago today according to a plaque

that's on display an oak-hulled packet bringing
porcelain clay was tripped in storms by jonah's
outstretched leg & left her crew to be engulfed
just half a furlong from the shore in seas as cold
& black as soulless eyes as cancer or shark attack

stormclouds steal impotent light of shrinking days
the hiss of prospero's bitter spells in requiem dirge
whip up the waves like cruel meringues which suck
the fledgling terns into the glacier gullet of a trough
both wide & deep enough to hide a million bodies in

## durante's brother

his face is a street-map of broken veins;
his nose, an aubergine, in certain light,
*worldly excesses*, he says, & *a cruel run
of luck with the women.* & when the priest
from st. dominic's talked about redemption
through a heavy mist of blackbush, danny
just smiled, cleared his throat as if to sing:

*this here bar is the house of our lord;
so kick off your work boots father
& shut the fuck up!*

## grey

ged has the head of a wildebeest
- today anyhow.

he is fucked off big-style
'cos *some twat* in safeway's car park
has let a trolley dent the wing of his car.

*probably a fuckin' mackem,*
he says, climbing into the fork-lift.

it is the type of afternoon
a man could paint himself grey
become invisible.

## follies

steve, her brother, is *staying neutral.*
he's just here to shift her gear.

he bends his legs, negotiates
the landing's odd geometry

& the last straining box of her intricate
follies heads out to the van.

so that's it then? onwards & upwards?
brave new worlds?

i suppose a last minute reconciliation
is out of the question?

a tall order even for them,
those agents of fortune dudes,
whoever the fuck they might be.

## praha 2004

the graves of josefov
huddle for warmth.
we place pebbles from home
on the grave of any
*zommerplag* or *kohn*.
the stones are barbed thorns,
a thousand rotten teeth
defying subsidence,
defying the kaddish's
last goodbyes.

# klezmer

the ashkenazi girl
fingers the black wood
of her clarinet,
each digit slender
as bean shoots,
as tendrils
negotiating
difficult spans,
broad reaches,
extended holds,
her lips wetting
the trembling reed,
savouring its resonance
like the ritual host.

## oh mother, where art thou?
(20.04.04, novosibirsk)

the familiar sulphur of burnt coal
hangs in neat strata

between spotlight glare
& cold tracks.

a stuttering tannoy bleats
the 3 am train is late,

the wind only
the weight of a child's breath

sickly, laboured,
bemoaning.

sparse moonlight
strings a cat's cradle

snaring the legs
of consumptive birch,

the bloodshot neon of the hotel sibir
scrawled in reverse

on the chemical workers' tenements,
each grime etched casement

a pomegranate cell,
a ruby in some despotic crown.

svetlana's vague ghost
sweeps leaves

on lenin road
& sergei weeps.

snowmelt congregates
at the refuge collection point,

a giant club-foot
in the tarmac's hollow.

the night-watchman
at the double-glazing factory

steps out from his box
hits the wall of frozen air.

his daughters dream in english,
his wife in silence,

& 4 time zones from here
our daisy has learnt to say no

& the concept of repetition:
baths, nappies and creamed root vegetables

all things rebutted
in the space of an hour.

# wake for an unborn child

a drunken harmonica
squeals with glee
& pale ghosts jig.

dark whisky rains
leaping like salmon
from chipped cups.

the tree is blighted,
red spot, mildew
& us childless.

a norse wind enunciates
the dead weight of absence.

## the butcher's craft

the butcher's wife is beautiful.
irish, i think, from that singing lilt.
hardly surprising he bagged such a catch,
a man with a trade, an ancient craft -
his deft knife skating on the rind,
his stitching immaculate.

later, in their humid bathrrom,
he double-checks a lump on her breast,
his strong hands reading the curves,
a tender smile masking fear,
the smell of meat still on his fingers.

## autumn in summer

morning affirmed
the clouds retreat

her mother nods, that's all,
eyes wide in simple endorsement

and the girl with perfect hands
plucks the first blackberry of the year

arrogant in its ripeness, each jet cell
puffed out like a squaddie's chest

indigo juice, warm as blood
clinging to her pallet like molasses.

this blackberry time
this season of the ghost

a woman with perfect hands
lays a yellow rose on her mother's grave

clears a season of weed, stands a while
remembering the sweetness of autumn in summer

## potts point, sydney, nsw.

*the cross* has much to bear:
its soul, untouching sex, the sweating
street, a rattle of speech in the perfume
of coffee, of green thai curry.

& down the breathless steps,
*the projects, woolloomooloo*, the arrival
sheds church-hollow, a stripped carcass,
history, bleached & flaking,

gulls chasing echoes in perfect sky,
a dog-fight in christmas heat:
I will carve my name on your chalky skin,
whisper remember me.

## shallow water

north stradbroke island, queensland

another fat bream ploughs a lazy furrow, mouthing a barrage
of silent profanity. fierce sun spearing the arc of her flank

every scale, the fresh sheen of shaved pewter. enter right,
the shadow-play shark's deadly geometry slaloming weed,

riding the barrel of an outstretched wave, the distance between us
well flighted spit & fused in the weld of fear and awe, exhale, incite

the breaking surf to dissipate the blood-scent on my hands, transform
the pasty bow of english legs to mangrove root, the tautness of my spastic

trunk into a trunk. I shaman, shallow water shape-shifter, shark-
whisperer, deceiver of the squalus, order of the lucky bastard, the fool

who fished at Amity, at dusk, in water made murky by the mud-crabs'
dance; what privilege this, to meet your killer in a dream and be awake.

## the marriage

*let's go to safeway*, she said.
*let's get married*, said he,
half asking, half telling
& all but drowned out
by the drone of the washer.
& she carried on with the shopping list
& he dreamed about a sunny hill,
a derelict temple, scorched white,
inhabited only by a family of doves.
& she asked if they needed cornflakes.
& he promised his love at the altar
of an unpronouncable goddess,
his entire body beaming with truth.
*do you need some more coffee?*
she said, & he answered, *i do,*
*with all the life in my heart, i do.*

& so they were married
between the cornflakes
& the soap-powder,
her not really knowing
& him knowing too well.

## surrealist marries cannabis plant
## in low-key ceremony

the happy couple
send a postcard home:

*dearest mother,*
*weather lovely.*
*have sold my kidneys*
*to a turkish surgeon.*

& him 'the rational one'.

once, in a phone box
near mansfield town centre
he forgot how to speak,
his entire past like chalk lines
fading in steady drizzle.

paulhino strums his flamenco guitar
& sylvia, at the listening-station,
intercepts a message from the fat controller:

*there but for the grace of god go i.*

# the restorer

he had once spent months
on the fractured smile
of some pre-raphaelite's dream,
a week of weeks on the calloused
hands of a shadowy dutch master,
a still-life apple ripe for re-invention -
re-set the tousled manes of nymphs & gods,
redressed the bleeding hands of christ
for the little sisters convent in lisburn.
always the mender, doctoring time,
each purposeful stroke, a cheat on the clock.
his tools of imitation becoming himself,
each measured sweep, each palette range,
a gloss of someone else's.

once, out of mischief,
he painted a welling tear
in the eye of a gleeful *comtesse*,
a single, blank concession
to the craftmanship of honesty.

## vermeer's dark parlour

all this culture makes you hungry!
i could eat a million fruit filled still-lives,
sink a gallon of that blood red wine
infused with the pewter
of the squire's ancient goblet!
*the dutch masters,* i'll say,
clearing my throat
in a simultaneous action,
*are so... urbane.*

baldy is stuffing his bake
& that barmaid looks anaemic.
then the bearded one speaks,
*pass the salt frederico,*
*this pasta has no taste.*

nuff said!

meanwhile,
in the general vicinity
of my elder brother's flat,
seagulls glide, curtains flap,
someone's angry tongue falls silent.

## score

my stroll to the shop for milk
had a catchy riff in eight bars,
slick & jazzy, incorporating traffic.

heading back to the flat i'm tailed
by a woman pushing a buggy.
the baby cries & she looks ominous.

i swerve around the post box & into the sun
& the band are ad-libbing now
more upbeat than ever & building to crescendo.

the silence comes as a perfect foil
& my key echoes in the chamber of the lock.
as i hurdle the junk mail, the draught
from the bedroom has the faintest trace of violins.

## exile

i bum a tab from andy as though never away,
nod at some smiling face over in the snugs.

i laugh at the tale of skinna's sheep-rustling.
i notice we are drinking at a different pace.

by last call we are silent, exhausted by the roll-call.
we buy kebabs, stumble home over the heap

the drizzle on our faces, like a thousand tiny kisses,
a thousand tears.

# let's call it morning

when you pulled on your tights
you looked a picture

leaning on the edge of morning.

i mention the beauty of it
& you blush

half hidden now
by the silk of your camisole.

## december song

a graceful eddy of frozen sand
slaloms like a mischievous cat
between the arch of foot & foot
& like a dull thrombosis ache
scales my calf to spread its grip

the cormorant spears the sorry sprat
air salt charged the hissing waves
slouched then proud & loosely coiled
like lids of sturdy pies on floured pins
put down their hands to break the fall

competing with the engine roar of wind
i sing a made-up song too loud & out
of tune it merges with the whinging gulls
the rogue bassoon of the fog horn boom
the beach as hollow as a christmas night

# kev

the beautiful woman
on the ashington bus
peels a tangerine
with great dexterity.
perfumes mingle, time moves
& kev tells the latest
of his new found friends
how he'd once been so hungry
he had eaten a candle,
how according to his nurse
he was 'more unpredictable
than a rabbit with a switch-blade'.
later, at the traffic lights
kev farts, loud & proud,
a stylised homage
to *findus crispy pancakes*
& the kids at the back
shake with laughter.
the pensioner adjacent
is less convinced,
is scared & disgusted
in the same lined face.
& the beautiful woman
on the ashington bus
who had peeled a tangerine
with great dexterity
smiled like florence nightingale
at some poor bastard
who had lost both his legs
to the roundness of a canonball.

## plain

over denwick, the sun, a burst yolk
spitting its gilt on slumped wheat,
painting sapphires on the magpie's flanks

cold basalt whalebacks on the beach,
a lime-washed tern surfing the thermals
& caedmon's portly ghost supping mead

finding philosophy in the movement of dunes,
bernicia's surrendered forts, fading cup stains
herding their summits like busy collies

the stuttering copse whispers a ballad,
conjures memories, bruised with dirt.
a father and his boy stop work for bait

watching the stars from a hole in the ground.

## northumbria

drizzle kissed
    the whining gull diluted
sea-washed bone sky-dome
    smudged cheviot bracken-bound
snow-melt & ram-skull
    king edwin's ghost stalks peewits
for a lonely feast
    & bloodstone bastles perfect rose
in flimsy light
    as pretty as cycladic moons.

## wave watcher

dropped to honkers
balanced like a frog
by a driftwood fire
he builds a see-saw
a crumbling whelk

a blunted razorshell
the fulcrum & deck
eyes blurred by cold
the dim stars rushing
to their next discovery

# the searchers

a daft dog shares the cold,
wrestling a stick too heavy
for it's neck, a fret anointed
union of shiverers of sifters
searchers of pebbles & wood

between us we could build a house
kept secret, in the sculpted lull
of long-haired dunes the gap
between exasperated sea & us
the distance of well-flighted spit.

# glass

all morning sand-pipers
spin and reel in milky fog,
rising in a synchronised skip
on the slow lap of the tide.
an old man collects sea-glass,
his shuffle meticulous,
his eyes fixed like an eagle's.

he drops each frosted jewel
carefully into a nap-sack.
there are whispers of senility
back at the allotments
& archie's glass hoarded
by the bean-canes like marner's gold.
occasionally, he is static, in reverence,

his bare feet, leather-skinned & salt-white,
sinking like picture-hall wurlitzers
into the sand. the ice mosaics
on the rippled floor, the double rainbow
slouched above the harbour, the dead seal
on the drift-line - swelled to a split,
like a fatty sausage too quickly fried.

# january song

there, like a cryptic clue to all our dumb histories,
the dog-shit of footprints head off into the distance

& yesterday's hockle has dried like sulphur
on the plateau of a traffic calming ramp.

the wind carries heartbreak, a swirl of chinese whispers,
a symphony of lover's names in the sighing of air-brakes.

of all glimpsed detail in winter's thin, ambivalent light,
only these are certainties: our skin will grow loose,

our bones melt.

## judgement day

it's baking hot. we regret wearing coats.
from the slit top-deck window of a 39 bus
a skinny, ginger kid in a *kappa* tracksuit
shouts *paki cunts* at two old arabs.
the gobful of *pepsi* he spits at them
blows back, narrowly misses our bags.
he mutters sorry when i stare. there is
a crusty glue-sore on his bottom lip &
his skin is overly pink, like a wax crayon.
his two fat mates obviously think he's cool.
they laugh their tits off at his every move,
taking tokes off the *regal kingsize* they'd
bummed just then from the pipe-cleaner
woman with bleached blonde hair. they
smoke it like a spliff, sucking 'til their
cheeks collapse & blowing mis-shaped
smoke-rings over our heads. they look
like urang-utangs, especially the ginger one.

## tell me again what she said

i had all but forgotten
her face,

our blunt goodbyes,
as black & irreparable
as her smeared mascara,
verse after verse
of unutterable truth,
her chorus of daggers
let fly, like a skyful
of starlings, as dense
as guinness.

the old man opposite
weaves another tale,
& me still unravelling
his parable of the talented.

tell me again what she said.

## car crime

*sum cunt's popped ya sidelight,* he said.
& they had.

a thousand diamonds scattered on the tarmac,
the glove compartment gaping, my A to Z
cowering by the clutch pedal, traumatised.

## summer flu

i like my new doctor.
he wears tee-shirts
to the surgery
& drives a ford fiesta.
he reminds me of my brother
in all his shy confidence
& tries too hard for laughs
when he really doesn't need to,
but he smiles with his eyes
& i like that in a man.

i have often thought
of my brother as a doctor
healing the rips
between me & my father
& sometimes my mother,
once even an uncle
at the birthday of an auntie,
when the truth was irresistible
& he took offence.

i like my new doctor.
his prescription is alternative.
when i visited him this morning
with a dose of summer flu
he recommended cheap greek wine
& a handful of nurofen
& then sounding once more
like the brother i rarely see now,
he told me to sleep
until i was well.

## the dinner party

one more mention of the william morris biography, verity
& i'll stick this steak-knife through your fucking heart!

did your mammy or your daddy never tell you?
that you just don't fuck with deranged anarcho-syndicalists,
especially when they're eating! we're the type of people
who'd have no hesitation in messing with the brake fluid
on your flashy new volvo! oh & let me guess verity,
the next subtle twist in your cosy conversation
will in some way make mention of your new labour
membership - how the herr blair bunch have brought back
the smile to the gleaming teeth of affluence.

& to think i once fancied you!
licked your calf muscles in sordid dreams!

you've as much charisma as a vacuum flask verity,
& less fucking brains. am i the only one who thinks that?
am i? does no one else feel the urge to kill?

cone on verity: the dado rails, tell us about your dado rails -
just fucking try it!

## english breakfast

wrestling the perfume of frying eggs,
a trace of whisky orbits *the sun*.

it is bastille day & the pale sky shrinks.
an ash-tray is slowly filling.

the old man with no fingers remembers
the shriek of the circular saw,

his belligerent jumper straining at the seams,
a leaking prostrate dampening his spirits.

he had once had a trial with blackburn rovers.
he is dying of something he cannot spell.

# interior

warrinilla, queensland

ahead of us, to infinity, the damp track:
an unstemmable trickle of blood, from &
to nowhere. & everywhere, the gagging
stench of dead or dying draws our tourist
eyes to road-kill: a small grey, curled
like a sleeping child & daubed
with an oil-slick of carrion greed. the birdcloud
explodes in feathery spores, their blade-grinder
screech walking on our graves. the carcass is
warm as dough from the day's gentle heat,
its slim wrists frozen skyward, splayed like a
frail aunt's arms in welcome, its open flank
pulsing with maggots. then dusk. the sun
plummeting like a dropped coin. only the
faint halo, now, of far-off traffic, the brilliant
stars - pin-pricks in deep velvet. we kiss.
somewhere northwards, an old man is tending
roses, plucking out suckers with strong fingers,
his dark singlet visible through sweat-wet shirt.
he is secretly shedding tears for a long-dead
lover, as his tired wife adds flour to the gravy.

# flood
cabbage tree creek, balgownie

all afternoon the trees whisper warnings
& news of antarctica's dreary gossip.

the sky ripens like a bruise
from quick-lime to grey flint,
grey flint to widow's veil
& solemn clouds tumble,
like a legion of clumsy children
down the step of the escarpment.

tonight, we will have no candyfloss sunset,
no clinked glasses or warm laughter
late on the veranda. only the chill lash
of relentless rain, as unwelcome
& unfriendly as cancer's cold greeting.

# the last illness

i knew as soon as you said
*we really have to talk.*

your face a grey seascape,
grim horizon looming,

your swan-neck posture
wielding ill-fortune,

like a tired old physician
beaten again by relentless nature.

your silent lips carrying word
of this, the last illness.

## last rites

burying a fiver in my palm, he goes all sage-like,
smiling at the union of our delicate fingers.
*there are no pockets on a shroud.*
each sparkle of passion in his casual eyes
uneasy lessons for the young to learn:
how a movie can end long before
the credits, how the dying can yearn
for the comfort of soil, of clinging fire.

## autumn

outside & above, sky, the colour of failure
a baby cries, hunger hardening her raw mouth

unwelcome autumn lifts another slate
grey boughs recoil & leaves submit

the old man with the cancer stare
discusses the narrowness of his bed

eyes loud, a carillon of hollow sorrow
the worst mask ever made, the most futile.

## veterans

okay, so you touched hendrix's
trouser leg at the isle of wight festival.
whoopee-fucking-doo!

the bass player from the uk subs
once gobbed right in my eye: but i'm
not making a song & fucking dance.

& before you even ask, comrade -
i have no interest whatsoever
in seeing your red vinyl copy
of *frampton comes alive*.

## sideburns

so who are you then, freddie,
to lecture on the aesthetics of facial hair?
the very man who had a stupid zapata
moustache himself when we first met!
the very man, freddie,
who thought he looked cool
with the fuck-off amish beard!
can you remember the seventies, fred?
let he who has not sinned
chuck the first frigging brick.

# crime & punishment

no man should live
to see his children
die before himself
today erect & stiff
an admiral plinthed

a slouch corrected
by monotone wind
alone like solomon
in painful thought
for eighteen nights

relentless dreams
have painted him
a lapwing's nest
sacked for sport
one gentle spring.

# drinking with dad

dad's are like bank managers:
they only understand you
in very brief bursts.
a fragile union.

belching out a bellyful of malt
& yeast, i conceded. *fair play*,
i said, *the model stakhanovite*
*i am not: but where comrade,*
*in this thankless town,*
*have your blisters got you?*

## november central southbound

katrina, as i have taken to calling her,
licks the city's drizzle from her upper lip,
& the footbridge at leyton
is bending over backwards to catch our attention,

moist & arching, like an unfranked stamp
steamed off, or a dying, land-locked fish.
& then, a moment of perfect congregation,
of aqualine clarity in the blur of a landscape:

how the fat bloke at stratford bears
a frightening resemblance to robespierre's death-mask;
how all our ageing fathers are slowly going mad,
have aligned themselves to theories

on the cyclical nature of history; how they
stockpile food covertly; how they've started
on the hull of a fibre-glass ark & nervously
watch the sky for big black clouds.

& the student from bethnal green,
whose *guardian* i read daily without his consent,
contemplates the power of a single well-used word:
how if white city was emerald

this irksome journey
might actually be worth it.

# uncle charlie goes ingmar bergman

they're the only things that bring me back.
weddings and funerals. mainly funerals.
if i had a quid for every shite co-op buffet
i'd sifted through of late, i could take you
to corsica. one more stale meringue, son,
& i'll give up the ghost myself,
just as a fucking protest.

# the last man

i am too sensitive to be a centre-back.
each attack stops my heart like an awkward question,
each panicked call of 'clear it!' like an oncoming car.
& it's hardly surprising that the last man in defence
always looks much older than he actually is.
but the manager is deaf to my *cris de coeur*
& reluctant to alter a winning team. he palms me off
with promises & praise, & usually i buy it, with my
appetite for eulogy & my vulnerable condition.

i get butterflies three days before kick-off,
have recurring dreams of underweighted back-passes
& headed own goals. i have become a mindless soldier,
conditioned to defend. i jump obediently at the captain's
noisy words, & dive in selflessly where few would dare.
i trip & kick in the name of victory, sacrifice my
gentleness for the good of the team. & i have grown
to pathologically resent forwards
for their complete lack of empathy.

& not just theirs: i hate ours more. i envy their goal tallies
& their penalty shouts, & their misguided wisdom from
the relative safety of the opposition's box. i often imagine
methods of cruel torture for our gobby midfielders or
our egocentric strikers, who speak through their arses,
& only then in words of one syllable.
it's not that i'm bitter, or a serious malcontent,
but i wasn't cut out for an unsung role,
& the crap they come out with would have galled
a fucking saint.

& however good a tackle is, however spectacular a scissor-kick
clearance, or a sweetly timed lunge to prod away the ball,
it's not a goal, & i'm rarely allowed to raise my arms or salute
the bench, & leap into the crowd to receive their adulation.
i have reconciled myself to inglorious duty, the bitter reality
that coach loads of travelling fans will never sing a chorus of
'one paulie summers'; but i wish they'd understand when they
jeer my hurried slices, or boo my frantic hoofs, that i'm not that
happy to be playing as last man, & i've told the boss repeatedly
that i really am too sensitive.

## poppy day

so what about jimmy? shot in the arse with a high velocity air rifle by sniffa's big brother, or little tommy, dowsed with lighter fuel, for a laugh, by pissed up skins; who even now speaks with a stutter? & the gleaming steel plate that's screwed to my skull, where glen dropped a brick from the top of the bridge in a daring re-enactment of a scene from zulu! & poor old robbo, who is no longer with us, squashed by a tankie playing chicken on the lines. or frenchy, who got it nesting for a kestrel's egg on the cold blue pylons. come wet november sundays, come armistice, will anyone remember, but us?

# newcastleton, spring 2004

high above the old kirk's
brittle boned spire
the hawk takes a finch on the wing.
angel eyed sky empty now,
the only evidence, down
spiralling like mauve snow

the whole brief thing
sublime tragedy
scored in my head
with wolfgang's requiem:
*confutatis, lacrimosa,*
*rex tremendae*
perhaps.

## on quarry moor

as frail light crumbles like dried leaves, like stale bread
the bell-pit crater is patient, a shallow bowl of quiet moss
hoarding its cache of rabbit shite muggies like inca gold

a manic cloud-crowd flirts as it flits, dirtied & distempered
a mob of hungry rooks circling harehope's empty barrows
& sheep tracks underscore the shivering lapwing's cat-call,

an ancient shepherd's secret bleats ducking the wind-blast
shell-shocked, tired, the lime-kiln slumps & ruffled lichen
cocks a curious ear to thirsty heather's crackling foot-fall.

as frail light crumbles like dead mortar, like poisoned soil
my father & his children, us, breathe deeply in the saccharine
air of home, of dusk, & build a cairn for ghosts with dirty nails.

## the comrades

every season brings change:
more empty seats for overcoats
& greasy caps, to prop up sticks.
their collars grow more loose,
their feet rattle in pristine shoes.

the incredible shrinking men
meet sundays for dominoes.
their fingers grip the ebony,
like brambles on unkempt graves.
they eye the kitty like preying cats,

faces receding to sharpened bone,
the skin of one-time double-chins
hangs paper-thin in breathless flags
& when they laugh, their straining necks
like pelicans remembering storms.

## another marlboro cowboy
## is dying of cancer

good question *amigo*!
good question.

how *do* i feel?

yesterday, as empty as a house
on the day you move out -
things echoed. today,
it's when frankie gets it
in *von ryan's express*,
or a speculative treble
goes down by a nose:

sorta anger & self-pity
in the same damp eye.

one for the road *compadre*?
one for the road...

# Acknowledgements

The author gratefully acknowledges the support and enthusiasm of all magazine and small press editors who have previously published any of the poems included in this collection.

Previous publications:
*140195* (Echo Room Press, Newcastle, 1995)
*Vermeer's Dark Parlour*
(Echo Room Press, Newcastle, 1996)
*Beer & Skittles* (Echo Room Press, Newcastle, 1997)
*The Last Bus* (Iron Press, Cullercoats, 1998)
*The Rat's Mirror* (Lapwing Press, Belfast, 1999)
*Cunawabi* (Cunawabi Publishing, London, 2003)

# about the author

Paul Summers was born in Blyth, Northumberland in 1967. He now lives in North Shields.

His work has appeared in print since the late Eighties and he has performed his work in Britain, Europe and Australia. He was a founding co-editor of the ground-breaking leftfield magazines *Billy Liar* and *Liar Republic* and a co-director of Liar Inc Ltd, responsible for facilitating countless creative projects across the North in educational and community contexts.

Paul Summers has also written for television, film and theatre and has collaborated with artists on mixed-media projects.

Home (in 3 bits), a collaboration with musician Dave Hull-Denholm was released in Spring 2006.

His first collection of poetry *The Last Bus* was published by Iron Press to critical acclaim, and the title sequence was included in the Forward Book of Poetry 1999.

## Praise for *The Last Bus*:

"Astute and sensitive powers of observation expressed through straightforward but genuinely poetic use of language." - Mike Parker, *Daily Star*

"Evocative power in mundane things"
- Alan Brownjohn, *Sunday Times*

"Bristlingly gifted" - *Dazed & Confused*

"Chilling and often funny, driven by love and anger, this is a striking testament to northern life in a time of dissolution and change" - Sean O'Brien, *Northern Review*

"Savagely accurate without ever sacrificing an appealing ironic humour" - *Poetry Quarterly Review*